WITHDRAWN

STATE PROFILES
KANSAS

BY ALICIA Z. KLEPEIS

BELLWETHER MEDIA • MINNEAPOLIS, MN

Blastoff! Discovery launches a new mission: reading to learn. Filled with facts and features, each book offers you an exciting new world to explore!

BLASTOFF! UNIVERSE

BLASTOFF! Beginners — GRADE K

BLASTOFF! READERS — GRADES 1-3

BLASTOFF! DISCOVERY — GRADE 4

This edition first published in 2022 by Bellwether Media, Inc.

No part of this publication may be reproduced in whole or in part without written permission of the publisher.
For information regarding permission, write to Bellwether Media, Inc., Attention: Permissions Department,
6012 Blue Circle Drive, Minnetonka, MN 55343.

Library of Congress Cataloging-in-Publication Data

Names: Klepeis, Alicia, 1971- author.
Title: Kansas / by Alicia Z. Klepeis.
Description: Minneapolis, MN : Bellwether Media, Inc., 2022. | Series: Blastoff! Discovery: State profiles | Includes bibliographical references and index. | Audience: Ages 7-13 | Audience: Grades 4-6 | Summary: "Engaging images accompany information about Kansas. The combination of high-interest subject matter and narrative text is intended for students in grades 3 through 8"– Provided by publisher.
Identifiers: LCCN 2021019691 (print) | LCCN 2021019692 (ebook) | ISBN 9781644873878 (library binding) | ISBN 9781648341649 (ebook)
Subjects: LCSH: Kansas–Juvenile literature.
Classification: LCC F681.3 .K58 2022 (print) | LCC F681.3 (ebook) | DDC 978.1–dc23
LC record available at https://lccn.loc.gov/2021019691
LC ebook record available at https://lccn.loc.gov/2021019692

Editor: Rebecca Sabelko   Designer: Kathleen Petelinsek

Printed in the United States of America, North Mankato, MN.

TABLE OF CONTENTS

A family arrives at Kaw Point Park in Kansas City.
The early morning summer air is damp and warm. They
stroll along a boardwalk and see both the Missouri and
Kansas Rivers. They then rent kayaks to explore the rivers
up close. The family watches a great blue heron snatch up
a fish.

KANSAS STATE CAPITOL

MONUMENT ROCKS

TALLGRASS PRAIRIE
NATIONAL PRESERVE

WILSON STATE PARK

KAW POINT

They head to the Kansas Speedway after lunch.
Colorful race cars whiz along the track. Near sunset,
they go ziplining at nearby Zip KC. The leaves seem
to glow against the sunset. Welcome to Kansas!

WHERE IS KANSAS?

Kansas is a rectangular state in the middle of the United States. It covers 82,278 square miles (213,099 square kilometers). Colorado sits to the west of Kansas. Nebraska is its northern neighbor. The Missouri River creates a jagged edge along the northeastern corner. Missouri is to the east. Oklahoma lies to the south.

Topeka is the state's capital. It is located in northeastern Kansas. The largest city is Wichita. It lies in the south-central part of the state.

COLORADO

N
W E
S

NEBRASKA

MISSOURI

MISSOURI
RIVER

KANSAS
CITY

TOPEKA ★

OVERLAND
PARK

OLATHE

KANSAS

WICHITA

OKLAHOMA

KANSAS'S BEGINNINGS

KANSA TRIBE

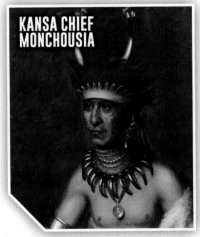

KANSA CHIEF MONCHOUSIA

People arrived in Kansas over 12,000 years ago. These first **settlers** were hunters and gatherers. Over time, they formed Native American groups including the Kansa, Osage, Pawnee, and Wichita tribes.

In 1541, Spanish explorers entered the area. French fur traders arrived in the 1700s. They exchanged goods with Native Americans. The U.S. gained Kansas in 1803 through the **Louisiana Purchase**. Beginning in 1830, the U.S. government forced many Native Americans into Kansas. But the state opened to white settlers in the 1850s. They pushed Native Americans into Oklahoma. Kansas became the 34th state in 1861. It also joined the **Union** in the **Civil War** that year.

NATIVE PEOPLES OF KANSAS

IOWA TRIBE OF KANSAS AND NEBRASKA

- Original lands in Iowa
- Many live in Kansas, Nebraska, and Oklahoma today
- Also called Ioway

KICKAPOO

- Original lands in northwestern Ohio, southern Michigan, Indiana, Illinois, Iowa, and Minnesota
- Many live in Kansas, Oklahoma, and Texas today

POTAWATOMI

- Original lands in Michigan
- Many live in Kansas, Oklahoma, parts of the Midwest, and Ontario, Canada, today

SAC AND FOX NATION

- Original lands in Michigan, Wisconsin, Iowa, and Missouri
- Many live in Kansas, Oklahoma, and Iowa today
- Also called Sauk (Sac) and Meskwaki or Mesquakie (Fox)

Kansas is known for its vast **plains**. Yet the state is not all flat. The Flint Hills are found in eastern Kansas. This area is mostly treeless and covered in bluestem **prairie**. Rivers such as the Kansas and Big Blue created **bluffs** in the northeast. Gentle hills and forests also cover this area.

The **Great Plains** make up the western half of the state.

BIG BLUE RIVER

KANSAS RIVER

N
W+E
S

FLINT HILLS
GREAT PLAINS

CASTLE ROCK

SPRING
HIGH: 65°F (18°C)
LOW: 41°F (5°C)

SUMMER
HIGH: 88°F (31°C)
LOW: 64°F (18°C)

FALL
HIGH: 67°F (19°C)
LOW: 43°F (6°C)

WINTER
HIGH: 42°F (6°C)
LOW: 21°F (-6°C)

°F = degrees Fahrenheit
°C = degrees Celsius

Kansas summers are hot and winters are cold. **Precipitation** falls throughout the year. The eastern part of the state is wetter than the west. Tornadoes have caused much damage in the state. **Droughts** sometimes affect Kansas as well.

KANSAS'S FUTURE: CLIMATE CHANGE AND WATER

As Kansas becomes drier and hotter from climate change, water resources are shrinking. Less rain is expected to fall in coming years. River water and groundwater will decrease. This may affect crops. Kansans may need to find more water sources.

AMERICAN BISON

Kansas is home to many kinds of animals. Bison graze on grasses as western hognose snakes slither in search of toads and small lizards. Nine-banded armadillos search for bugs. Lesser prairie-chickens and scaled quails feast on seeds in the shortgrass prairies of the Great Plains. These birds can be hard to spot in their grassy habitat.

Black-tailed jackrabbits scamper through their home ranges. They can run as fast as 40 miles (64 kilometers) per hour! Owls and hawks swoop down from cottonwood trees to snatch up plains pocket gophers.

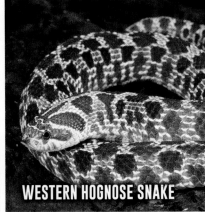

WESTERN HOGNOSE SNAKE

LESSER PRAIRIE-CHICKEN

GREAT HORNED OWL

BLACK-TAILED JACKRABBIT

KANSAS'S CHALLENGE: UNWANTED FISH

Originally from Asia, silver carp are negatively affecting some of Kansas's waterways. Many live in the Kansas River. They often reduce the population of fish such as bass. Government programs are working to remove silver carp from Kansas water bodies.

NINE-BANDED ARMADILLO

Life Span: up to 20 years
Status: least concern

nine-banded
armadillo range =

LEAST CONCERN	NEAR THREATENED	VULNERABLE	ENDANGERED	CRITICALLY ENDANGERED	EXTINCT IN THE WILD	EXTINCT
▲						

13

Around 3 million people live in Kansas. About three out of four Kansans live in **urban** areas. The state's largest city is Wichita. But Overland Park, Kansas City, Olathe, and Topeka are also big cities.

OVERLAND PARK

TOPEKA

FAMOUS KANSAN

Name: Janelle Monáe
Born: December 1, 1985
Hometown: Kansas City, Kansas
Famous For: A Grammy-nominated musical artist and award-winning actress known for her role in the film *Hidden Figures*

More than 4 out of 5 Kansans are white. Their **ancestors** are European, often coming from Britain and central Europe. The second-largest group of people is Hispanic Americans. A small number of Asian Americans and Black or African Americans live in the state. Around 1 out of 100 Kansans are Native American. The largest group of **immigrants** in Kansas comes from Mexico. Others are from India, Vietnam, Guatemala, and China.

THE KEEPER OF
THE PLAINS

The Wichita people first settled in Wichita in 1863. Soon after, white settlers began to arrive. J.R. Mead founded a trading post along the Arkansas River in 1864. The area became the city of Wichita in 1870. It was an important center for cattle drives. Meatpacking and aircraft **manufacturing** have been major industries since the early 1900s.

16

Today, Wichita is home to the country's biggest dinosaur theme park. The city has over 100 miles (161 kilometers) of walking and bicycle paths! Wichita has a growing population of people with a Latino background. They have influenced many Latin American restaurants and grocery stores.

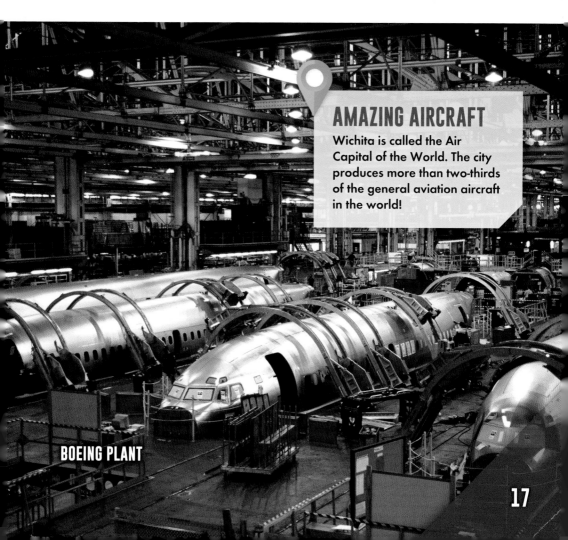

AMAZING AIRCRAFT

Wichita is called the Air Capital of the World. The city produces more than two-thirds of the general aviation aircraft in the world!

BOEING PLANT

17

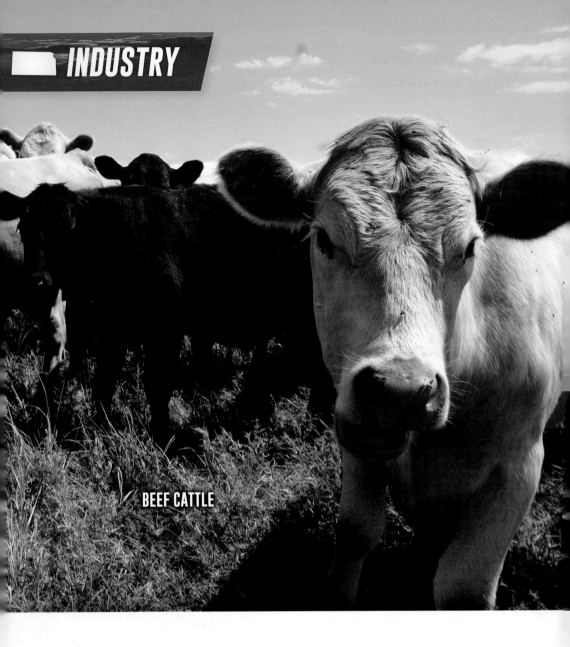

BEEF CATTLE

Farming and ranching have been important to Kansas's economy since its early days. The state is one of the nation's biggest producers of wheat, grain **sorghum**, and beef. It is also a leader in flour milling. Nearly 7 out of 10 Kansans have **service jobs**. Many work in finance or transportation services.

Manufacturing makes a lot of money for Kansas. On average, this industry employs more people in Kansas than in other U.S. states. Many transportation goods are produced throughout the state.

AWESOME AMUSEMENT RIDES

Chance Rides is an amusement ride manufacturer in Wichita. They make roller coasters, Ferris wheels, and more for parks like Universal Studios and Six Flags.

INVENTED IN KANSAS

ELECTRIC HAIR CLIPPERS

Patent Approved: 1915

Inventor: Samuel Coffman

ROTARY DIAL

Patent Approved: 1892

Inventor: Almon Strowger

ICEE

Date Invented: late 1950s

Inventor: Omar Knedlik

EARLY HELICOPTER

Date Invented: 1909

Inventors: William Purvis and Charles Wilson

AN UNUSUAL SCHOOL LUNCH

Decades ago, the U.S. Department of Agriculture sent large amounts of beans to school cafeterias. Cooks used the beans to make chili. They also served cinnamon rolls to encourage kids to eat the chili. Now this combo is a favorite lunch!

Many popular Kansas foods are related to its beef production. Steak, hamburgers, and barbecue ribs are just a few examples. *Bierocks* are dough pockets with ground meat and cabbage inside. Kansans also eat many kinds of bread, such as deep-fried grebble or a flatbread called lefse.

BIEROCKS

A famous dessert in Kansas is a spicy cookie called the peppernut. Kansas dirt cake is a sweet treat made with Oreo cookies and vanilla pudding. Pies are a **traditional** dessert amongst farmers. Coconut cream is a favorite flavor at many restaurants.

PEPPERNUT COOKIES

SPOON BREAD

4
SERVINGS

Have an adult help you make this recipe.

INGREDIENTS

4 cups milk

1 cup yellow cornmeal

1 1/4 teaspoons salt

2 tablespoons butter, plus more for serving

4 eggs

DIRECTIONS

1. Preheat the oven to 400 degrees Fahrenheit (204 degrees Celsius).

2. In a large pan, heat the milk on the stove over medium heat. Slowly stir in the cornmeal and salt. Keep stirring and cooking until the mixture becomes thick and smooth. Turn down the heat and cook for another 5 minutes, stirring constantly. Add the butter, and remove the pan from the heat.

3. In a medium-sized bowl, whisk the eggs until completely blended. Pour these into the cornmeal mush.

4. Pour the batter into a greased 8-by-8-inch pan. Bake, uncovered, for 45 to 55 minutes until puffy and golden brown.

5. Serve right away with plenty of butter. Enjoy!

CROP ART

FIELDS AS CANVASES

Crop artist Stan Herd creates artworks out of farmers' fields. These masterpieces are best seen from a rooftop or a plane. They show images like a vase of flowers or American folk heroes.

The wide-open space of Kansas provides a lot of recreational activities. Several ranches offer horseback riding to visitors. Many Kansans go fishing on the state's rivers and lakes. People cross-country ski at the Flint Hills Nature Trails during the winter. In warmer weather, golf is popular on courses throughout Kansas.

Soccer lovers support Kansas's only professional sports team, Sporting Kansas City. College basketball games draw huge crowds. The Kansas Jayhawks and Kansas State Wildcats are wildly popular. Kansans enjoy the performing arts in many cities. Wichita hosts events from Broadway shows to monster truck jams.

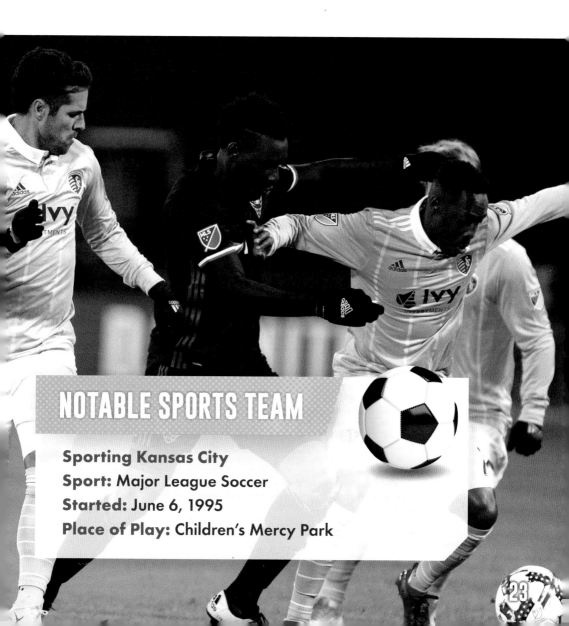

NOTABLE SPORTS TEAM

Sporting Kansas City
Sport: Major League Soccer
Started: June 6, 1995
Place of Play: Children's Mercy Park

RODEO

Rodeos are a popular tradition in Kansas. Each February, Kansas State University holds a college rodeo. Participants compete at bull riding, barrel racing, and other cowboy skills. In June, music lovers flock to the Heartland Stampede for a three-day country music festival.

OZTOBERFEST

Dorothy from *The Wonderful Wizard of Oz* comes from Kansas. Each October, the town of Wamego hosts OZtoberFEST. There are costume contests and many other Oz-some activities!

Hundreds of thousands of people attend the Kansas State Fair each September. There are farm exhibits and live music. Other fun State Fair traditions include pig racing and butter sculptures. Fall events include the Columbus Hot Air Balloon Regatta and the Oakley Corn Festival. Kansans celebrate their traditions and festivals throughout the year!

COLUMBUS HOT AIR BALLOON REGATTA

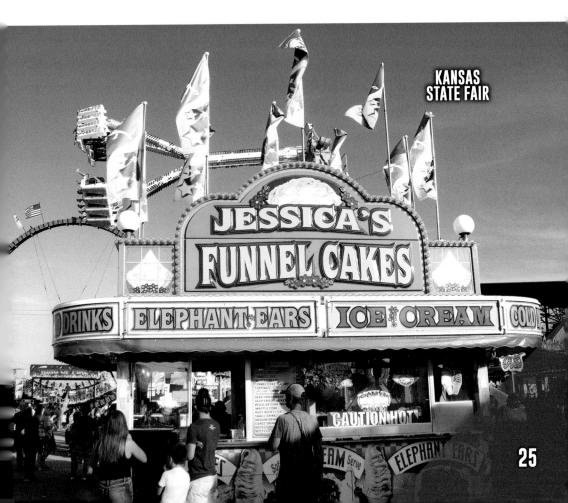

KANSAS STATE FAIR

JESSICA'S FUNNEL CAKES

DRINKS ELEPHANT EARS ICE CREAM COLD

CAUTION HOT

KANSAS TIMELINE

1541

Francisco Vázquez de Coronado is the first European explorer to arrive in the area

1830

The U.S. government starts forcing Native Americans into Kansas from their original lands in the eastern U.S.

1803

Kansas becomes part of the United States through the Louisiana Purchase

1861

Kansas becomes the 34th state in the U.S. and joins the Union in the Civil War

26

1930s

Southwest Kansas, along with other areas of the Great Plains, becomes a dust bowl when severe drought and wind damage farmland

2007

One of the most destructive tornadoes in recorded history levels most of the town of Greensburg

2018

Sharice Davids is the first female Native American from Kansas to serve as a U.S. Representative

1990

Joan Finney is elected the first female governor of Kansas

2017

The Starbuck wildfire, the largest in Kansas history, burns more than 500,000 acres (2,023 square kilometers) near Wichita

Nicknames: The Sunflower State, The Wheat State, The Jayhawker State

State Motto: *Ad Astra Per Aspera* (To the Stars Through Difficulties)

Date of Statehood: January 29, 1861 (the 34th state)

Capital City: Topeka ★

Other Major Cities: Wichita, Kansas City, Overland Park, Olathe

Area: 82,278 square miles (213,099 square kilometers); Kansas is the 15th largest state.

Population

2,937,880
(2020)

STATE FLAG

The background of the Kansas flag is dark blue. At the top center is a sunflower, the official state flower. In the middle of the flag is the state seal. It features a settler with plow horses and a cabin. Above the scene, 34 stars represent Kansas being the 34th state in the U.S. The state's name runs across the bottom center of the flag.

INDUSTRY

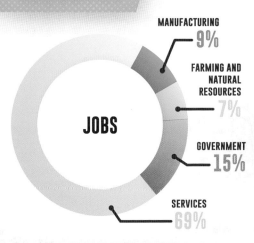

JOBS

MANUFACTURING
9%

FARMING AND NATURAL RESOURCES
7%

GOVERNMENT
15%

SERVICES
69%

Main Exports

wheat

beef

aircraft

machinery

Natural Resources
fertile soil, oil, natural gas, limestone

GOVERNMENT

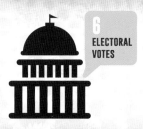

6 ELECTORAL VOTES

Federal Government

4 REPRESENTATIVES | **2** SENATORS

USA

KA

State Government

125 REPRESENTATIVES | **40** SENATORS

STATE SYMBOLS

STATE FLOWER
SUNFLOWER

STATE BIRD
WESTERN MEADOWLARK

STATE ANIMAL
AMERICAN BISON

STATE TREE
COTTONWOOD

29

GLOSSARY

ancestors—relatives who lived long ago

bluffs—cliffs or steep banks that often overlook a body of water

Civil War—a war between the Northern (Union) and Southern (Confederate) states that lasted from 1861 to 1865

droughts—long periods of dry weather

Great Plains—a region of flat or gently rolling land in the central United States

immigrants—people who move to a new country

Louisiana Purchase—a deal made between France and the United States; it gave the United States 828,000 square miles (2,144,510 square kilometers) of land west of the Mississippi River.

manufacturing—a field of work in which people use machines to make products

plains—large areas of flat land

prairie—a large, open area of grassland

precipitation—water that falls to the earth as rain, snow, sleet, mist, or hail

service jobs—jobs that perform tasks for people or businesses

settlers—people who move to live in a new, undeveloped region

sorghum—related to a tropical grass often grown for grain or animal feed

traditional—related to customs, ideas, or beliefs handed down from one generation to the next

Union—related to the group of Northern states that fought to keep the country together during the Civil War; the Union fought against the Confederacy.

urban—related to cities and city life

TO LEARN MORE

AT THE LIBRARY

Bailer, Darice. *What's Great About Kansas?* Minneapolis, Minn.: Lerner Publications, 2016.

Gregory, Josh. *Kansas.* New York, N.Y.: Children's Press, 2019.

Heinrichs, Ann. *Kansas.* Mankato, Minn.: Childs World, 2017.

ON THE WEB

FACTSURFER

Factsurfer.com gives you a safe, fun way to find more information.

1. Go to www.factsurfer.com.

2. Enter "Kansas" into the search box and click 🔍.

3. Select your book cover to see a list of related content.

INDEX